A Mixed Bag Of Funny Poems - Author Unknown

Compiled & Edited by

David Sollis

TAP Publishing UK

Copyright © 2014 for this collection by **TAP P**ublishing UK
(www.TAPPublishing.uk)

Compiled and Edited by David Sollis

ISBN: 978-0-9573175-1-2

Preface

For as long as I can remember, I've been captivated by language and in particular the sounds of spoken words. My formative years were in a bi-lingual setting, so it doesn't matter to me what language is being spoken. All dialects have their own distinctive qualities, cadence, patterns, pulse, character and beauty. I don't believe that any one language is superior in any way.

As a child in the 1970's I would listen to the radio and get lost in the rhythm, melody and the word-smithery of the lyrics of the songs I heard. Quite often I would latch onto a single word that I liked the sound of and would repeat it to myself incessantly, so that I could play with it's delivery and structure.

Mrs. Jarman my first English Language teacher was a major influence in my discovery of rhyming verse. The contagious enthusiasm with which she read poetry in class affected me deeply. I still remember word for word several pieces of nonsense verse she read in class, some of which are included in this collection. She had a particular penchant for light verse and would have the whole class laughing out loud during her recitals. The sheer joy and emotion she invoked as she read, I've not experienced since.

Some of my favourite poems have been penned anonymously and I can recall and recite them at will. I'd be willing to bet that you can do this too. You may not realise it, but just about everybody knows some anonymous poetry, as most nursery rhymes have no attributed author. Or else their author has been long since forgotten, as they originated in a time before putting words in print was common practice.

Over the years I have accumulated a hefty collection of poetry books, which I add to from time to time. In my opinion there has always been something lacking in this collection (until now). There are many anthologies available for any genre and poet imaginable, but there are very few books dedicated solely to anonymous poems. During my research I only found one, a collection by Richard Bentley published in London in 1850. None of its contents have made it into this collection.

If, an individual poet were responsible for all the poems ever published with ANON noted as author, they would be the most prolific and long lived poet on the planet. This means I have been spoilt for choice for works to include and narrowing the selection to a reasonable number suited to a book such as this has been a very difficult process, but a labour of love. As there are a considerable number of poems that did not make the cut, but that nevertheless have merit, it is possible that other volumes may follow (depending on the success of this one of course).

If I'm honest the limerick is probably my favourite poetic form. This affection is obviously shared with ANON as it provided one of the richest hunting grounds for ANON works. Perhaps it's the sometimes bawdy, puerile or obscene nature of the limerick that results in people not wanting to be associated with their own work. Maybe this is also why they appeal so strongly to me. Anyway, with only limited space, I've had to curtail the number in this book (which was very difficult). But who knows, I may squeeze a few more in a future edition.

I've attempted to structure the verse in a logical sequence by grouping poems together by theme. This offers the reader the opportunity to dip in at any point to satiate their cravings for a particular topic. Or you can just read cover to cover of course and explore fully the delights this collection has to offer.

I hope you enjoy reading this book as much as I've enjoyed collating the poems within it.

David Sollis

Copyright Note: The editor has used his best endeavors to establish whether there is a legal right to be associated as the copyright owner for any of the works in this book. As far as he can ascertain, for all works included in this collection, none exists. However, if you believe he has included copyright material without permission, please contact the publisher by e-mail: permission@tappublishing.uk to rectify the situation by due acknowledgement or removal from future editions.

Table of Contents

Tall Stories

The Farting Contest

I'll tell you a story that is sure to please,
Of a great farting contest at Burton-on-Tees
Where all the best arses paraded the field,
To compete in a contest for various shields.

Some tighten their arses and fart up the scale,
To compete for a cup and a gallon of ale.
While others whose arses are biggest and strongest,
Compete in the section for loudest and longest.

Now this years event had drawn quite a large crowd,
And the betting was even on Mrs. MacLeod.
For it had appeared in the evening edition,
That this lady's arse was in perfect condition.

Now, old Mrs. Jones had a perfect backside,
Half a forest of hairs with a wart on each side.
And she fancied her chances of winning with ease,
Having trained on a diet of cabbage and peas.

The Vicar arrived and ascended the stand,
And thus he addressed this remarkable band.
"The contest is on as is shown in the bills,
We've precluded the use of injections and pills."

Mrs. Bindle arrived amid roars of applause,
And promptly proceeded to pull off her drawers,
For though she'd no chance in the farting display,
She'd the prettiest bottom you'd see this day.

Now, young Mrs. Pothole was backed for a place,
Though she'd often been placed in the deepest disgrace
By dropping a fart that had beaten the organ,
And the poor Vicar, old Jonathon Morgan.

Anon

The ladies lined up at the signal to start,
And winning the toss, Mrs. Jones took first fart
The people around stood in silence and wonder,
While her wireless announced gale warnings and thunder.

Now, Mrs. MacLeod reckoned nothing of this,
She'd had some weak tea and was all wind and pride.
So she took up her place and her arse opened wide,
But unluckily shit... and was disqualified.

Then young Mrs. Pothole was called to the front,
And started by doing a wonderful stunt.
She took a deep breath and clenching her hands,
She blew the whole roof off the popular stands.

That left Mrs. Bindle, who shyly appeared,
And smiled at the clergy who lustily cheered.
And though it was reckoned her chances were small,
She let out a winner, out-farting them all.

With hands on her hips, she stood farting alone,
And the crowd stood amazed at the sweetness of tone.
And the clergy agreed without hindrance or pause,
And said, "First, Mrs. Bindle... now pull up your drawers!"

But with muscles well tensed and legs full apart,
She started a final and glorious fart.
Beginning with *Chopin* and ending with *Wing*
She went right up the scale to *God Save the King*.

She went to the rostrum with maidenly gait,
And took from the panel, a set of gold plate.
Then she turned to the Vicar with sweetness sublime
And smilingly said, "Come up and see me some time!"

Johnny Sands

A man whose name was Johnny Sands
Had married Betty Haig
And though she brought him gold and lands,
She proved a terrible plague.

For oh, she was a scolding wife,
Full of caprice and whim.
He said that he was tired of life,
And she was tired of him!
And she was tired of him!

Said he, "Then I shall drown myself,
The river runs below."
Said she, "Pray do, you silly elf,
I wished it long ago!
I wished it long ago!"

"For fear that I should courage lack
And try to save my life
Pray tie my hands behind my back."
"I will!" replied his wife.
"I will!" replied his wife.

She tied them fast, as you may think
And when securely done,
"Now stand," said she, "Upon the brink,
And I'll prepare to run.
And I'll prepare to run."

All down the hill his loving bride
Now ran with all her force,
To push him in... he stepped aside
And she fell in, of course.
And she fell in, of course.

Now splashing, dashing like a fish,
"Oh save me, Johnny Sands!"
"I can't my dear, though much I wish,
For you have tied my hands.
For you have tied my hands."

Billy The Kid

Billy was a bad man
And carried a big gun,
He was always chasing women
And kept 'em on the run.

He shot men every morning
Just to make a morning meal –
If his gun ran out of bullets
He killed them with cold steel.

He kept folks in hot water,
And he stole from many a stage,
When his gut was full of liquor
He was always in a rage.

But one day he met a man
Who was a whole lot badder –
And now he's dead –
And we ain't none the sadder.

Hilda Hose

This is the tale of Hilda Hose
Who had a phosphorescent nose
Which sent out quite a glow before her
Reminding one of dawn's aurora.
And people meeting her at night
Would comment on it's ruddy light
And Hilda said, if she heard,
'Ruddy' was a well picked word.
She hated to be thought a freak
And cursed her large and crimson beak.
Especially it terrified her
If motorists drew up beside her
And waited there with words obscene
For Hilda's nose to turn to green.
At last, abandoning restraint,
She camouflaged her nose with paint
But once again she missed the bus
Because the paint was luminous.
And people thought it out of place
To meet a nose without a face.
And Hilda hated being teased,
About the fireworks when she sneezed.
But now, at last, I'm glad to say
Some better luck has come her way,
For though the crimson glow remains
Miss Hilda Hose no more complains.
For Sanctioned by the A.R.P. *
She stands outside a surgery
And with her phosphorescent snout
She guides the patients in and out.

* A.R.P. - Air Raid Patrol

Anon

The Barking-Creek Bell-Ringer's Daughter

The Barking Creek bell-ringer's bell it gets rung
When the fog lies thick on the water,
Though it's not of the Barking Creek bell my song's sung
But of the Barking Creek bell-ringer's daughter.

Now she was so lovely, so fair and so squat
That conductors fell off of their buses
As she walked down Cable Street bearing on top
Her bath full of live octopuses.

And all down her back from shoulder to thigh
Their tentacles hung down in tresses,
As sweetly she'd sing, "Won't you cough up and buy
My octopus, live octopuses?"

Now one day in August the sunshine was spread
On her wares that she proudly was bearing,
And the blowflies all glittered and buzzed round her head
Like the halos that angels are wearing.

As on the embankment her stock she laid out
In that far from salubrious quarter,
She aroused the wild passions of Algernon Stout
An unemployed Billingsgate porter.

Now Stout was a villain who wallowed in crime
Who lived under some derelict barges
And the day being hot, was laid out on the slime
Where the Barking Creek sewer discharges.

He crouched on the crust as the maiden drew nigh
Her petticoats all of a-splatter.
He licked his fat lips then, suddenly, like
A wild rhino-sore-arse, flew at her.

His head hit her first in a cloud of black dust
And the bath took off like a rocket
They crumpled and crashed 'til they broke through the crust
To the mud underneath which was clotted.

She pushed a large handful all slimy and green
Down his gob like a mouthful of jelly,
Then the bath full of octopus fell on the scene
Upside down on top of the melee.

Beneath it they struggled but Stout never knew
The danger to which he was liable
An octopus, slyly, did stealthily glue
Its sucker upon his left eyeball.

Now vainly Stout struggled to loosen its grip
And attempted the monster to throttle
When his eye came away with a pop and rip
With the sound like a cork from a bottle.

When Algernon spied he was only one-eyed
He was filled with distraught irritation
And grabbed the poor octopus by its inside
As a weapon of flag-e-olation.

The octopus turned inside out with a gulp
As Stout's actions got even distraughter
He sliced them all up and beat to a pulp
The Barking Creek bell-ringer's daughter.

Now there's some literati what's going to complain
That a moral should here be appended
Whilst others, as surely, will loudly maintain
That it's high time the bloody thing ended.

But all you bum critics take notice from me
If you're of the feminine gender,
That in Barking today, there's a vacancy
For a lady-like octopus vendor.

Anon

The Story Of Euphemia

[The children are sitting at Nanny's knee in the nursery as she tells them a charming bed-time tale.]

Now children, lend an ear or two,
For I've a tale to tell to you.
Concerning one Euphemia Pratt
(back in, chin up... don't slouch like that!).
No child's conduct was more abstemious;
Temper milder than Euphemia's,
A perfect child, full of grace,
Who always walked at walking pace.
Until one day (Oh!, don't do that...)
A fateful day for Family Pratt,
When Great Aunt Maude, and Uncle Hugh
Had come to spend a day or two.
They were expected to arrive
At roughly twenty-five to five,
And this they did with punctuality,
Knowing something of the locality.
Mama said, "Auntie, how-do-you-do?...
How nice you look and you too, Hugh."
Upon which Uncle Hugh sat down,
And with a low, lugubrious frown,
Began to tell a tale of wealth,
Of testaments and fading health.
Euphemia meanwhile was sitting,
Silently as was befitting,
Absent-minded, still and pale,
As her Uncle told his tale.
He talked with studied, stern monotony,
Of houses, gardens, botany.
Talked till nearly ten past eight,
Of duties, deeds, estates probate.
And then it was... (Oh children, hearken)
As the skies began to darken
That suddenly, and with no warning,
Euphemia... started... yawning!

She yawned but once, then yawned again,
She yawned and yawned nine times or ten.
She yawned so far, she yawned so wide,
Her gums and tonsils gaped inside.
"Gracious me!", cried Aunt Maude...
"I do believe the child is bored!"
Then crashing through the window there,
Came the great 'Yawn-Widener',
Hair on end, and mouth so grim
(Oh children, cringe... the sight of him).
For he's the one who comes in rage,
To children of a certain age,
Who, without the slightest warning,
Interrupt a speech with yawning.
He seized Euphemia by the teeth,
One hand above, one hand beneath.
He caught her yawn, and then began;
As all the best 'Yawn-Wideners' can,
To widen, stretch, enlarge her yawn.
Her lips were split, her throat was torn
And with a loud, triumphant shout...
He turned Euphemia . . inside out!
This done, he turned and bowed his head
And left and not a word he said.
Mama said, "Gracious me, oh dear
that this should happen, this in here.
Papa perceived Mama's distress,
And called the maid to clear the mess.
While Uncle Hugh surveyed the scene,
And said, "This incident has been
A grim reminder to us all,
Of all the things that can befall
Those who, without warning,
Interrupt a speech with yawning.
"Don't you agree, Aunt Maude?", he said,
But Great Aunt Maude alas... was dead!

Anon

It's A Sad, Sad Story

We're all in dreadful trouble down in our house,
Such an awful state of things you never saw.
For Mother's gone and put us all in mourning,
And I can't imagine what she's done it for.
I know the baby's coughing rather badly
And our parrot died of grief a week ago,
And so today I said to mother, sadly
"Mother dear, why are you weeping so?"
She raised her curly head...
And took my hand and said...

It's a sad, sad story...
A terrible tale of woe,
And it breaks my heart to tell you
What happened so long ago.
But it's just one year
Since your Papa was taken away,
So we've all put on our mourning
And we're all feeling sad today.

"Mother dear," I whispered, "tell me true
Our Father's story, wipe away your tears.
Was he taken from us unexpected?...
Or had you known the awful truth for years?
Dad must have had a decent situation,
He brought us lots of gifts from time to time
And though he must have spent long spells away, Ma,
To leave, for us, cannot have been a crime."
But she wept all the more...
And whispered as before...

"It's a sad, sad story...
A terrible tale of woe,
And it breaks my heart to tell you
What happened so long ago.

11

But it's just one year
Since your Papa was taken away,
So we've all put on our mourning
And we're all feeling sad today."

"Mother, though I'm young, I think in Heaven,
The angels will take pity on your pain.
Dad's term in purgatory will soon be over
And they will send him back to us again."
And though the words I said were meant to comfort
They only seemed to add to poor Ma's grief,
And in a voice so low I scarce could hear her,
She murmured , "Time is not the only thing,
I tried to tell you why,
I tried dear, not to cry...

It's a sad, sad story...
A terrible tale of woe,
And it breaks my heart to tell you
What happened so long ago.
But it's just one year
Since your Papa was taken away,
So we've all put on our mourning...
'Cos he comes out again today."

The Vulture

[Parody of Edgar Allan Poe's *The Raven* - Published in *Graham's Magazine* 1853]

Once upon a midnight chilling, as I held my feet unwilling
O'er a tub of scalding water, at a heat of ninety-four;
Nervously a toe in dipping, dripping, slipping, then out-skipping,
Suddenly there came a ripping whipping, at my chamber's door.
" 'Tis the second-floor," I muttered, "flipping at my chamber's door -
Wants a light - and nothing more!"

Ah! distinctly I remember, it was in the chill November,
And each cuticle and member was with influenza sore;
Falt'ringly I stirred the gruel, steaming, creaming o'er the fuel,
And anon removed the jewel that each frosted nostril bore,
Wiped away the trembling jewel that each reddened nostril bore,
Nameless here for evermore!

And I recollect a certain draught that fanned the window curtain
Chilled me, filled me with a horror of two steps across the floor,
And, besides, I'd got my feet in, and a most refreshing heat in,
To myself I sat repeating- "If I answer to the door-
Rise to let the ruffian in who seems to want to burst the door,
I'll be [damned]" that and something more.

Presently the row grew stronger; hesitating then no longer,
"Really, Mr. Johnson, blow it! - your forgiveness I implore
Such an observation letting slip, but when a man's just getting
Into bed, you come upsetting nerves and posts of chambers' door,
Making such a row, forgetting" - Spoke a voice beyond the door:
"It isn't Johnson" - nothing more!

Quick a perspiration clammy bathed me, and I uttered "Dammy!"
(Observation wrested from me, like the one I made before)
Back upon the cushions sinking, hopelessly my eyes, like winking,
On some stout for private drinking, ranged in rows upon the floor,
Fixed - and on an oyster barrel (full) beside them on the floor,
Looked and groaned, and nothing more.

Open then was flung the portal, and in stepped a hated mortal,
By the moderns called a VULTURE (known as Sponge in days of yore),
Well I knew his reputation! cause of all my agitation -
Scarce a nod or salutation changed, he pounced upon the floor;
Coolly lifted up the oysters and some stout from off the floor,
Helped himself, and took some more!

Then this hungry beast untiring fixed his gaze with fond admiring
On a piece of cold boiled beef I meant to last a week or more,
Quick he set to work devouring - plates, in quick succession, scouring -
Stout with every mouthful showering - made me ask, to see it pour,
If he quite enjoyed his supper, as I watched the liquid pour;
Said the Vulture, "Never more."

Much disgusted at the spacious vacuum by this brute voracious
Excavated in the beef--(he'd eaten quite enough for four) -
Still I felt relief surprising when at length I saw him rising,
That he meant to go surmising, said I, glancing at the door -
"Going? well, I won't detain you--mind the stairs and shut the door -"
-"Leave you, Tompkins! never more."

Startled by an answer dropping hints that he intended stopping
All his life--I knew him equal to it if he liked, or more -
Half in dismal earnest, half in joke, with an attempt at laughing,
I remarked that he was chaffing, and demanded of the bore,
Asked what this disgusting, nasty, greedy, vile intrusive bore,
Meant in cloaking "Never more."

But the Vulture not replying, took my bunch of keys and trying
Sev'ral, found at length the one to fit my private cupboard door;
Took the gin out, filled the kettle; and with a sang froid to nettle
Any saint, began to settle calmly down the grate before,
Really as he meant departing at the date I named before,
Of never, never more!

Then I sat engaged in guessing what this circumstance distressing
Would be likely to result in, for I knew that long before
Once (it served me right for drinking) I had told him that if sinking
In the world, my fortunes linking to his own, he'd find my door
Always open to receive him, and it struck me now that door
He would pass, perhaps never more!

Suddenly the air was clouded, all the furniture enshrouded
With the smoke of vile tobacco--this was worse than all before;
"Smith!" I cried (in not offensive tones, it might have been expensive,
For he knew the art defensive, and could coster-mongers floor);
"Recollect it's after midnight, are you going? - mind the floor."
Quoth the Vulture, "Never more."

"Smith!" I cried (the gin was going down his throat in rivers flowing),
"If you want a bed, you know there's quite a nice hotel next door,
Very cheap - I'm ill - and, joking set apart, your horrid smoking
Irritates my cough to choking. Having mentioned it before,
Really, you should not compel me - Will you mizzle - as before?"
Quoth the Vulture, "Never more."

"Smith!" I cried, "that joke repeating merits little better treating
For you than a condemnation as a nuisance and a bore;
Drop it, pray, it isn't funny; I've to mix some rum and honey -
If you want a little money, take some and be off next door;
Run a bill up for me if you like, but do be off next door."
Quoth the Vulture, "Never more."

"Smith!" I shrieked - the accent humbler dropping, as another tumbler
I beheld him mix, "be off! you drive me mad – it's striking four.
Leave the house and something in it; if you go on at the gin, it
Won't hold out another minute. Leave the house and shut the door -
Take your beak from out my gin, and take your body through the door!
Quoth the Vulture, "Never more!"

And the Vulture never flitting, still is sitting, still is sitting,
Gulping down my stout by gallons, and my oysters by the score;
And the beast, with no more breeding than a heathen savage feeding,
The new carpet's tints unheeding, throws his shells upon the floor.
And his smoke from out my curtains, and his stains from out my floor,
Shall be sifted never more.

Limericks

The Limerick

The limerick packs laughs anatomical
Into space that is quite economical,
But the good ones I've seen
So seldom are clean
And the clean ones so seldom are comical.

Young Lady Of Joppa

There was a young lady of Joppa
Who came a society cropper.
She went to Ostend
With a gentleman friend-
And the rest of the story's improper.

In Later Years

The enjoyment of sex, although great
Is in later years said to abate.
This well may be so,
But how would I know?
I'm now only seventy-eight.

Anon

Young Lady Of Ryde (1)

There was a young lady of ryde,
Who ate some green apples and died.
The apples fermented
Inside the lamented,
And made cider inside her inside(s).

Young Lady Of Ryde (2)

There was a young lady of Ryde
Who was carried far out by the tide.
Cried a man-eating shark,
"How's this for a lark?
I knew that the Lord would provide."

I Sat Next To The Duchess At Tea

I sat next to the Duchess at tea.
It was just as I feared it would be:
Her rumblings abdominal
Were simply phenomenal,
And everyone thought it was me.

Barmaid Of Sale

On the breasts of a barmaid in Sale
Were tattooed the prices of ale;
And on her behind
For the sake of the blind
Was the same information in Braille.

Young Lady Of Tottenham

There was a young lady of Tottenham,
Who'd no manners, or else she'd forgotten 'em;
At tea at the vicar's
She tore off her knickers
Because, she explained, she felt 'ot in 'em.

Said An Ape

Said an ape as he swung by his tail
To his offspring both female and male,
"From your children, my dears,
In a couple of years
May evolve a professor at Yale."

Anon

A Young Lady Named Gloria

There was a young lady called Gloria
Who was had by Sir Gerald Du Maurier
And then by six men
And Sir Gerald again
And the band of the Waldorf-Astoria.

A Young Artist Called Saint

There was a young artist called Saint
Who swallowed some samples of paint.
All shades of the spectrum
Flowed out of his rectum
With a colorful lack of restraint.

Poor Harry

When Daddy and Mum got quite plastered,
And their shame had been thoroughly mastered,
They told their boy, Harry:
"Son, we never did marry.
But don't tell the neighbours, you bastard."

Old Man Of Darjeeling

There was an old man from Darjeeling,
Who boarded a bus bound for Ealing.
He saw on the door:
'Please don't spit on the floor',
So he stood up and spat on the ceiling.

A Young Fellow Named Hyde

A simple young fellow named Hyde
In a funeral procession was spied.
When asked, "Who is dead?"
He tittered an said,
"I don't know. I just came for the ride."

Old Parson Of Fratton

There was an old person of Fratton
Who would go to church with his hat on.
"If I wake up," he said,
"With a hat on my head,
I will know that it hasn't been sat on."

Anon

Sea-Serpent

A sea-serpent saw a big tanker,
Bit a hole in her side and then sank her.
It swallowed the crew
In a moment or two,
And then picked it's teeth with the anchor.

Old Man Of Blackheath

There was an old man of Blackheath,
Who sat on his set of false teeth;
Said he, with a start,
"O Lord, bless my heart!
I've bitten myself underneath!"

Don Of Divinity

A complacent old Don of Divinity
Used to boast of his daughter's virginity:
"They must have been dawdlin',
The students of Magdalen-
It couldn't have happened at Trinity."

Bored With Harrison

I'm bored to extinction with Harrison.
His limericks and puns are embarrassing.
But I'm fond of the bum,
For, though dull as they come,
He makes me feel bright by comparison.

A Young Curate Of Kew

There was a young curate of Kew
Who kept a tom cat in a pew.
He taught it to speak
alphabetical Greek,
But it never got further than μ.

A Lady Dining At Crewe

A lady while dining at Crewe
Found an elephant's whang in her stew.
Said the waiter, "Don't shout,
Or wave it about,
Or the others will all want one too."

Anon

The Wizard Of Oz

The fabulous Wizard of Oz
Retired from his racket because,
What with up-to-date science,
To most of his clients
He wasn't the Wizard he was.

Three Little Owls

There were three little owls in a wood,
Who sang hymns whenever they could.
What the words were about,
One could never make out,
But one felt it was doing them good.

There Was An Archdeacon

There was an Archdeacon who said:
"May I take off my gaiters in bed?"
But the Bishop said: "No,
Wherever you go
You must wear them until you are dead."

President Ford

In the years of President Ford
Decorum and calm were restored.
He did nothing hateful
For which we were grateful
But terribly, terribly bored.

Lady Of Riga

There was a young lady of Riga
Who smiled as she rode on a tiger;
They returned from the ride
With the lady inside,
And the smile on the face of the tiger.

Old Man Of Madrid

There was an old man of Madrid
Who ate sixty-five eggs for a quid.
When they asked, "Are you faint?"
He replied, "No I ain't,
But I don't feel as well as I did."

Anon

Lady Of Lynn

There was a young lady of Lynn,
Who was so uncommonly thin
That when she essayed
To drink lemonade
She slipped through the straw and fell in.

Thrombosis

If intercourse gives you thrombosis
And continence causes neurosis,
I'd rather expire
Fulfilling desire
Than live in a state of psychosis.

Maud

There was a young lady called Maud,
A sort of society fraud.
In the parlor, 'tis told,
She was distant and cold,
But on the verandah, my Gawd!

A Famous Theatrical Actress

A famous theatrical actress
Played best in the role of malefactress.
Yet her home-life was pure
Except, to be sure,
A scandal or two just for practice.

Young Man Of Ghent

There once was a young man of Ghent
Whose tool was so long that it bent.
To save himself trouble
He put it in double,
And instead of coming, he went.

A Bridge Engineer

A bridge engineer, Mr. Crumpett,
Built a bridge for the good River Bumpett.
A mistake in the plan
Left a gap in the span,
But he said, "Well, they'll just have to jump it."

Anon

Young Lady Of Twickenham

There was a young lady of Twickenham
Whose boots were too tight to walk quickenham.
She bore them awhile,
But at last, at a stile,
She pulled them both off and was sickenham.

Alice

There was a young lady called Alice
Who peed in a Catholic chalice.
The Padre agreed
It was done out of need
And not out of Protestant malice.

Titian

When Titian was mixing brown madder,
His model was posed up a ladder.
Said Titian, "That position
Calls for coition,"
So he lept up the ladder and had her.

Siberian Monk

There was a young monk from Siberia
Whose morals were very inferior.
He did to a nun
What he shouldn't have done
And now she's a Mother Superior.

Young Australian

There was a young man of Australia
Who painted his ass like a dahlia.
The drawing was fine
And the painting divine
But the aroma—that was the failure.

The Plumber Of Leigh

There was a young plumber of Leigh
Was plumbing a maid by the sea.
Said the maid, "Cease your plumbing,
I think someone's coming."
Said the plumber, still plumbing, "It's me."

Bather

A bather whose clothing was strewed
By winds that left her quite nude
Saw a man come along
And, unless I am wrong,
You expected this line to be rude.

Pretty Young Thing

A pretty young thing from St Paul's
Wore a newspaper gown to a ball.
The dress caught on fire
And burned her attire
Front page, sporting section and all.

The Garden Of Eden

In the Garden of Eden lay Adam
Complacently stroking his madam,
And loud was his mirth
For he knew that on earth
There were only two balls - and he had 'em.

Faith Healer

There was a faith-healer of Deal
Who said, "Although pain isn't real,
        If I sit on a pin
        And it punctures my skin,
I dislike what I don't think I feel."

Young Lady Of Wantage

There was a young lady from Wantage
Of whom the town clerk took advantage.
        Said the borough surveyor:
        "Indeed you must pay 'er.
You've totally altered her frontage."

Lancelot

There was a young fellow called Lancelot
Whom his neighbors all looked on askance a lot.
        Whenever he'd pass
        A presentable lass,
The front of his pants would advance a lot.

Anon

The Family Stein

There's a wonderful family called Stein:
There's Gert and there's Ep and there's Ein.
Gert's poems are bunk,
Ep's statues are junk,
And no-one can understand Ein.

34

Education

OIC

I'm in a 10der mood 2day
& feel poetic, 2;
4 fun I'll just – off a line
& send it off 2 U.

I'm sorry you've been 6 o long;
Don't B disconsol8;
But bear your ills with 42de,
& they won't seem so gr8.

Spelling

Beware of heard, a dreadful word
That looks like beard and sounds like bird.
And dead: it's said like bed, not bead;
For goodness' sake, don't call it deed!
Watch out for meat and great and threat.
(They rhyme with suite and straight and debt.)
A moth is not a moth in mother,
Nor both in bother, broth in brother.

More Spelling

If an S and an I and an O and a U with an X at the end spells Sioux,
And an E and a Y and an E spells eye -
Pray what is a speller to do?
If an S and an I and a G and a H and an E and a D spells sighed,
Pray what is there left for a speller to do but -
To go and commit Sioux-eye-sighed?

Anon

Getting Information Out Of Pa

My pa he didn't go to town
    Last evening after tea,
But got a book and settled down
    As comfy as could be.
I'll tell you I was offul glad
    To have my pa about
To answer all the things I had
    Been tryin' to find out.

And so I asked him why the world
    Is round instead of square,
And why the piggies' tails are curled,
    And why don't fish breathe air?
And why the moon don't hit a star,
    And why the dark is black,
And just how many birds there are,
    And will the wind come back?

And why does water stay in wells,
    And why do June bugs hum,
And what's the roar I hear in shells,
    And when will Christmas come?
And why the grass is always green,
    Instead of sometimes blue,
And why a bean will grow a bean
    And not an apple, too?

And why a horse can't learn to moo,
    And why a cow can't neigh?
And do the fairies live on dew,
    And what makes hair grow gray-
And then my pa got up an' gee!
    The offul words he said,
I hadn't done a thing, but he
    Jest sent me off to bed.

Homework Lover

I love to do my homework,
It makes me feel so good.
I love to do exactly
As my teacher says I should.

I love to do my homework,
I never miss a day.
I even love the men in white
Who are taking me away.

A Student's Prayer

Now I lay me down to rest,
I pray I pass tomorrow's test.
If I should die before I wake,
That's one less test I'll have to take.

The Moron

See the happy moron,
He doesn't give a damn!
I wish I were a moron -
My God! Perhaps I am!

Money

Going On An Errand

A pound of tea at one and three
And a pot of raspberry jam
Two new laid eggs a dozen pegs
And a pound of rashers of ham.

I'll say it over all the way
And then I'm sure not to forget
For if I chance to bring things wrong
My Mother gets in such a sweat.

A pound of tea at one and three
And a pot of raspberry jam
Two new laid eggs a dozen pegs
And a pound of rashers of ham.

There in the hay the children play
They're having such fine fun
I'll go there too that's what I'll do
As soon as my errands are done

A pound of tea at one and three
A pot of er new laid jam
Two raspberry eggs with a dozen pegs
And a pound of rashers of ham.

There's Teddy White flying his kite
He thinks himself grand I declare
I'd like to make it fly up sky high
Ever so much higher than the old church spire

And then - but there

A pound of three at one and tea
A pot of new laid jam
Two dozen eggs, some raspberry pegs
And a pound of rashers of ham.

Anon

Now here's the shop outside I'll stop
And run my orders through again
I haven't forgot - it's better not
It shows I'm pretty quick that's plain.

A pound of tea at one and three
A dozen of raspberry ham
A pot of eggs with a dozen pegs
And a rasher of new laid jam.

To A Lawyer

Trapped by my neighbour in his clover,
Three pigs I fee'd you to recover.
Before the court you gravely stand,
And stroke your wig and smooth your hand;
Then, taking up the kingdom's story,
You ope your case with Alfer's glory;
Of Norman William's curfew bell
And Couer de Lion's prowess tell;
How through the ravaged fields of France
Edwards and Henries shook the lance;
How great Eliza o'er the main
Pursu'd the shatter'd pride of Spain,
And Orange broke a tyrant's claim.
All this, good sir, is mighty fine;
But now, an please you, to my swine!

The Bishop's Mistake

The Bishop glanced through his window pane
On a world of sleet, and wind, and rain,
When a dreary figure met his eyes
That made the bishop soliloquize.

And as the Bishop gloomily thought
He ordered pen and ink be brought,
Then 'Providence Watches' he plainly wrote
And pinned the remark to a ten bob note.

Seizing his hat from his lordly rack
And wrapping his cloak around his back,
Across the road the bishop ran
And gave the note to a shabby man.

That afternoon was the bishop's "at home"
When everyone gathered beneath his dome,
Curate and canon from far and near
Came to partake of the bishop's cheer.

There in the good old bishop's hall
Stood a stranger lean and tall,
"Your winnings, my lord" he cried. "Well done
Providence Watches, at ten to one."

It is to be noted on Sunday next
The bishop skillfully chose his text,
And from the pulpit earnestly told
Of the fertile seed that returned tenfold.

Anon

The Village Burglar

Under the spreading gooseberry bush
The village burglar lies;
The burglar is a hairy man
With whiskers round his eyes.

He goes to church on Sundays;
He hears the Parson shout;
He puts a penny in the plate
And takes a shilling out.

A Musician And Dance Teacher Who Stole Money Collected For A Musical Publication

His time was quick, his touch was fleet;
Our gold he neatly finger'd:
Alike alert with hand and feet,
His movements have not linger'd.
Where lies the wonder of the case?
A moment's thought detects it:

His practice has been thorough-bass,
A chord will be his exit.
Yet, while we blame his hasty flight,
Our censure may be rash.
A traveller is surely right
To change his notes for cash.

To A Living Author

Your comedy I've read, my friend,
And like the half you pilfered best;
Be sure the piece you yet may mend –
Take courage, man, and steal the rest.

That Drained Your Purse

I change, and so do women too;
But I reflect—which women seldom do.
Tobacco is a filthy weed,
That from the devil doth proceed;
That drains your purse, that burns your clothes,
That makes a chimney of your nose.

Advice To Copywriters

When your client's hopping mad
Put his picture in the ad.
If he still should prove refractory
Add a picture of his factory.

Services Rendered

It seems I impregnated Marge
So I do rather feel, by and large,
Some cash should be tendered
For services rendered,
But I can't quite decide what to charge.

Life & Death

I'm Fine Thank You

There is nothing the matter with me.
I'm as healthy as I can be.
I have arthritis in both my knees
And when I talk, I talk with a wheeze.

My pulse is weak, and my blood is thin
But I'm awfully well for the shape I'm in.
Arch supports I have for my feet
Or I wouldn't be able to be on the street.

Sleep is denied me night after night,
But every morning I find I'm all right.
My memory is failing, my head's in a spin
But I'm awfully well for the shape I'm in.

The moral is this, as my tale I unfold,
That for you and me who are growing old,
It's better to say "I'm fine" with a grin
Than to let folks know the shape we are in.

How do I know that my youth is all spent?
Well, my "get up and go" just got up and went.
But I really don't mind when I think with a grin
Of all the grand places my "get up" has been.

Old age is golden, I've heard it said;
But sometimes I wonder as I get into bed
With my ears in the drawer my teeth in a cup,
My eyes on the table until I wake up.

Ere sleep overtakes me, I say to myself,
"Is there anything else I could lay on the shelf?"
When I was young my slippers were red,
I could kick my heels over my head

Anon

When I was older my slippers were blue,
But I still could dance the whole night through.
Now I am old, my slippers are black,
I walk to the store and puff my way back.

I get up each morning and dust off my wits
And pick up the paper and read the obits.
If my name is still missing, I know I'm not dead
So I fix me some breakfast and go back to bed.

What Makes A Dad

God took the strength of a mountain,
The majesty of a tree,
The warmth of a summer sun,
The calm of a quiet sea,
The generous soul of nature,
The comforting arm of night,
The wisdom of the ages,
The power of the eagle's flight,
The joy of a morning in spring,
The faith of a mustard seed,
The patience of eternity,
The depth of a family need,
Then God combined these qualities,
When there was nothing more to add,
He knew His masterpiece was complete,
And so,

He called it ... Dad

Little Boys

Little boys come in all shapes and sizes,
Shy and adventurous, full of surprises,
With misshapen halos and mischievous grins,
Small dirty faces, and sweet, sticky chins.

They'll keep you so busy, and yet all the while
Nothing can brighten the world like their smile.
And no greater treasure has brought homes more joy
Than a curious, active, and lovable boy!

Sisters

If only I hadn't had sisters
How much more romantic I'd be
But my sisters were such little blisters
That all women are sisters to me.

What Is A Basket?

"Oh, Daddy dear, what is a basket?"
Said a youthful and mischievous elf:
"All baskets, me boy, are children of joy.
In fact you're a basket yourself."

Anon

Shoes

My father has a pair of shoes
So beautiful to see.
I want to wear my father's shoes.
They are too big for me.

My baby brother has a pair
As cunning as can be.
My feet won't go into that pair.
They are too small for me.

There's only one thing that I can do
Till I get small or grown.
If I want to have some fitting shoes
I'll have to wear my own.

5 Little Brothers

5 little brothers set out together
To journey the livelong day,
In a curious carriage all made of leather
They hurried away, away!
One big brother, and 3 quite small,
And one wee fellow, no size at all.

The carriage was dark and none too roomy,
And they could not move about;
The 5 little brothers grew very gloomy,
And the wee one began to pout,
Till the biggest one whispered: "What do you say?
Let's leave the carriage and run away!"

So out they scampered, the 5 together,
And off and away they sped;
When somebody found the carriage of leather,
Oh my, how she shook her head!
Twas her little boy's shoe as everyone knows,
And the 5 little brothers were 5 little toes.

How To Treat Grandma

When Grandma visits you, my dears,
Be good as you can be;
Don't put hot waffles in her ears,
Or beetles in her tea.

Don't sew a pattern on her cheek
With worsted or with silk;
Don't call her naughty names in Greek,
Or spray her face with milk.

Don't drive a staple in her foot,
Don't stick pins in her head;
And, oh, I beg you, do not put
Live embers in her bed.

These things are not considered kind;
The worry her, and tease -
Such cruelty is not refined
It always fails to please.

Be good to Grandma, little chaps,
Whatever else you do;
And then she'll grow to be - perhaps -
More tolerant of you.

Monday's Child

Monday's child is fair in face,
Tuesday's child is full of grace,
Wednesday's child is full of woe,
Thursday's child has far to go,
Friday's child is loving and giving,
Saturday's child works hard for its living;
And a child that is born on a Christmas day,
Is fair and wise, good and gay.

Trifles

The massive gates of Circumstance
Are turned upon the smallest hinge,
And thus some seeming pettiest chance
Oft gives our life its after-tinge.

The trifles of our daily lives,
The common things scarce worth recall,
Whereof no visible trace survives,
These are the mainstrings, after all.

The Busy Man

If you want to get a favor done
By some obliging friend,
And want a promise, safe and sure,
On which you may depend,
Don't go to him who always has
Much leisure time to plan,
But if you want your favor done,
Just ask the busy man.

The man with leisure never has
A moment he can spare,
He's always "putting off" until
His friends are in despair.
But he whose every waking hour
Is crowded full of work
Forgets the art of wasting time,
He cannot stop to shirk.

So when you want a favor done,
And want it right away,
Got to the man who constantly
Works twenty hours a day.
He'll find a moment, sure, somewhere,
That has no other use.
And help you, while the idle man
Is framing an excuse.

Anon

A Man Of Words

A man of words and not of deeds
Is like a garden full of weeds
And when the weeds begin to grow
It's like a garden full of snow
And when the snow begins to fall
It's like a bird upon the wall
And when the bird away does fly
It's like an eagle in the sky
And when the sky begins to roar
It's like a lion at the door
And when the door begins to crack
It's like a stick across your back
And when your back begins to smart
It's like a penknife in your heart
And when your heart begins to bleed
You're dead, and dead, and dead indeed.

Going To The Dogs

My granddad, viewing earths worn cogs,
Said things were going to the dogs;
His granddad in his house of logs,
Said things were going to the dogs;
His granddad in the Flemish bogs,
Said things were going to the dogs;
His granddad in his old skin togs,
Said things were going to the dogs;
There's one thing that I have to state
The dogs have had a good long wait.

Mithing Tooth

I'm having trouble thpeaking,
thinthe I lotht my middle tooth.
Jutht yethterday my tooth wath fine-
today it wiggled loothe.

At firtht I thought it thilly,
when my tooth fell out today,
but no one theems to underthtand
a thingle word I thay.

I athked my mom to clothe the door,
she said "I cannot make it.
The door does not like wearing clothes;
it's happier when naked."

I athked if I could have a mouthe,
I promithed I would feed it,
"Another mouth to feed?" she athked,
"I'm certain we don't need it!"

I wonder if you underthtand
the thircumthtanthe I'm in.
I told her I wath feeling thick.
She thaid "you're looking thin."

At latht she thaw how mad I wath,
ath if I may thtop breathing.
She laughed and thaid she didn't mean it-
she wath only teething.

Anon

Toil

Toiling rejoicing, sorrowing,
So I my life conduct.
Each morning see some job begun,
Each evening see it chucked.

I Thought If

If I thought that a word of mine
Perhaps unkind and untrue,
Would leave it's trace on a loved one's face,
I'd never speak it….
Would you?

If I thought that a smile of mine
Might linger the whole day through
And lighten the heart with a heavier part,
I'd not withhold it….
Would you?

Wounded Cupid

Cupid as he lay among
Roses, by a Bee was stung.
Whereupon in anger flying
To his Mother, said thus crying;
"Help! O help! your Boy's a dying."
"And why, my pretty Lad", said she?
Then blubbering, replied he,
"A winged Snake has bitten me,
which Country people call a Bee."
At which she smil'd; then with her hairs
And kisses drying up his tears:
"Alas!" said she, "my Wag! if this
such a pernicious torment is:
Come, tell me then, how great's the smart
Of those, thou woundest with thy Dart!"

A Woman's Looks

A woman's looks
Are barbed hooks,
That catch by art
The strongest heart,
When yet they spend no breath.
But let them speak,
And sighing break
Forth into tears,
Their words are spears
That wound our souls to death.
The rarest wit
Is made forget,
And like a child
Is oft beguiled
With Love's sweet-seeming bait.
Love with his rod
So like a god
Commands the mind
We cannot find,
Fair shows hide foul deceit.
Time, that all things
In order brings,
Hath taught me now
To be more slow
In giving faith to speech:
Since women's words
No truth affords,
And when they kiss
They think by this
Us men to overreach.

Anon

Beauty

As a beauty I'm not a great star,
There are others more handsome by far,
  But my face, I don't mind it,
  Because I'm behind it,
'Tis the folks in the front that I jar.

Woman

A Woman is a book, and often found
To prove far better in the Sheets than bound:
No marvel then why men take such delight
Above all things to study in the night.

On Seeing A Lady's Garter

Why blush, dear girl, pray tell me why?
You need not, I can prove it;
For though your garter met my eye,
My thoughts were far above it.

A Taking Girl

She took my hand in sheltered nooks,
She took my candy and my books,
She took the lustrous wrap of fur,
She took those gloves I bought for her.
She took my words of love and care,
She took my flowers, rich and rare,
She took my time for quite awhile,
She took my kisses, made so shy-
She took, I must confess, my eye,
She took whatever I would buy.
And then she took another guy.

Pleased And Innocent

I gently touched her hand: she gave
A look that did my soul enslave;
I pressed her rebel lips in vain:
They rose up to be pressed again.
Thus happy, I no farther meant,
Than to be pleased and innocent.

On her soft breasts my hand I laid,
And a quick, light impression made:
They with a kindly warmth did glow,
And swelled and seemed to overflow.
Yet, trust me, I no farther meant,
Than to be pleased and innocent.

On her eyes my eyes did stay:
O'er her smooth limbs my hands did stray;
Each sense was ravished with delight,
And my soul stood prepared for flight.
Blame me not if at last I meant
More to be pleased than innocent.

Anon

An Original Love Story

He struggled to kiss her. She struggled the same
To prevent him so bold and undaunted;
But as smitten by lightning, he heard her exclaim
"Avaunt, Sir!" and off he avaunted.

But when he returned, with the fiendishest laugh,
Showing clearly that he was affronted,
And threatened by main force to carry her off,
She cried "Don't!" and the poor fellow donted.

When he meekly approached, and sat down at her feet,
Praying aloud, as before he had ranted,
That she would forgive him and try to be sweet,
And said "Can't you!" the dear girl recanted.

Then softly he whispered, "How could you do so?
I certainly thought I was jilted;
But come though with me, to the parson we'll go;
Say, wilt thou, my dear?" and she wilted.

The Nameless Maiden

A Maid, I dare not tell her name;
For fear I should disgrace her,
Tempted a young man for to come
One night for to embrace her.
When at the door he made a stop, he made a stop,
Then she lay still, and snoring cry'd,
"The latch will up, the latch will up."

This young man, hearing of her words,
Pull'd up the latch and entered;
But in the room unfortunately
To her mother's bed he ventured.
When the poor maid was sore afraid,
And almost dead, and almost dead;
Then she lay still, and snoring cry'd,
"To the truckle bed, to the truckle bed."

Unto the truckle bed he went,
But as this youth was a-going,
The unlucky cradle stood in his way,
Which had almost spoil'd his wooing.
When after this the maid he spy'd, the maid he spy'd,
Here she lay still, and snoring cry'd,
"To th'other side, to th'other side."

Unto the other side he went,
To show the love he meant her;
Pull'd off his clothes courageously,
And fell to the work he was sent for.
And the poor maid made no reply, made no reply,
But she lay still, and snoring cry'd,
"A little too high, a little too high."

This lusty lover half ashamed,
Of her gentle admonition,
He thought to charge her home again,
As e'er a girl could wish him.
"Why now my love, I'm right I know, I'm right I know."
Then she lay still, and snoring cry'd,
"A little too low, a little too low."

But by mistake, at length this youth
His business so well 'tended,
He hit the mark so cunningly,
He defy'd all the world to mend it.
"Well now, my love, I'm right I swear, I'm right I swear."
Then she lay still, and snoring cry'd,
"Oh there! just there! O there! just there!"

Bridget Bearwell

In Woolstonecraft's page, Bridget Bearwell was skill'd
And her fancy with novel inventions was fill'd
But Bridget improv'd on Miss Wool- stonecraft's plan,
And projected some small revolution in man.
"Tis plain," she exclaim'd, "that the sexes should share,
In each other's employments, amusements and care.
I'm taught in man's duties and honors to join,
And, therefore, let man be partaker of mine:
Since to share with my husband in logic I'm fit
In classical lore, mathematics, and wit;
In return, he shall yield the pot, kettle, and ladle,
And unite in the charge of the kitchen and cradle."

Unfortunate Miss Bailey

A captain bold from Halifax who dwelt in country quarters,
Betrayed a maid who hanged herself one morning in her Garters.
His wicked conscience smited him, he lost his Stomach daily,
And took to drinking Ratafia while thinking of Miss Bailey.

One night betimes he went to bed, for he had caught a Fever;
Says he, "I am a handsome man, but I'm a gay Deceiver."
His candle just at twelve o'clock began to burn quite palely,
A Ghost stepped up to his bedside and said "Behold Miss Bailey!"

"Avaunt Miss Bailey!" then he cries, "your Face looks white and mealy."
"Dear Captain Smith," the ghost replied, "you've used me ungenteelly;
The Crowner's Quest goes hard with me because I've acted frailly,
And Parson Biggs won't bury me though I am dead Miss Bailey."

"Dear Corpse!" said he,"since you and I accounts must once for all close,
There really is a one pound note in my regimental Small-clothes;
I'll bribe the sexton for your grave." The ghost then vanished gaily
Crying, "Bless you, Wicked Captain Smith, Remember poor Miss Bailey."

Poor But Honest

She was poor but she was honest,
Victim of the squire's whim:
First he loved her, then he left her,
And she lost her honest name.

Then she ran away to London,
For to hide her grief and shame;
There she met another squire,
And she lost her name again.

Anon

See her riding in her carriage,
In the park and all so gay;
All the nibs and nobby persons
Come to pass the time of day.

See the little old-world village
Where her aged parents live,
Drinking the champagne that she sends them;
But they never can forgive.

In the rich man'd arms she flutters,
Like a bird with broken wing;
First he loved her, then he left her,
And she hasn't got a ring.

See him in the splendid mansion,
Entertaining with the best,
While the girl that he has ruined,
Entertains a sordid guest.

See him in the House of Commons,
Making laws to put down crime,
While the victims of his passions
Trails her way through mud and slime.

Standing on the bridge at midnight
She says: "Farewell, blighted Love."
There's a scream, a splash – Good Heavens!
What is she a-doing of?

Then they drag her from the river,
Water from her clothes they wrang,
For they thought that she was drownded;
But the corpse got up and sang:

"It's the same the whole world over,
It's the poor that get's the blame,
It's the rich that gets the pleasure.
Isn't it a blooming shame?"

Little Lessons

The love I bear you, dearest,
Would make the sweetest tale,
We'd sail upon a sea of bliss,
And I would lift the sail.
Our happiness would be sublime,
Surpassing tongue or pen.
You may as well learn things from me,
As to learn from other men.

"Oh! you have touched me deeply"
The young thing whispered low.
He pleaded: "Come! oh! come with me."
She could not answer: "No."
She said: "I'll be your pupil."
And softly added then:
"I may as well learn things from you
As to learn from other men."

They dined alone that evening,
And the young man got his wish.
They even broke the unwritten law
Of: "Nevaire before zee feesh."
At half-past three, next morning,
He staggered home again.
She had taught him tricks he never knew,
That she'd learned from other men.

The German Of Lessing

You hesitate if you shall take a wife.
Do as your father did – live single all your life.

Anon

Matrimony

To wed, or not to wed-that is the question;
Whether 'tis happier in the mind to stifle
The heats and tumults of outrageous passion,
Or with some prudent fair in solemn contract
Of matrimony join. To have-to hold-
No more-and by that "have" to say we end
The heart-ache, and the thousand love-sick pangs
Of celibacy-t'were a consummation
Devoutly to be wished. In nuptial band
To join till death dissolves-ay, there's the rub;
For in that space what dull remorse may come,
When we have taken our solemn leave of liberty,
Must give us pause. There's this respect
That slacks our speed in suing for a change:
Else, who would bear the scorns and sneers which bachelors
When aged feel—the pains and fluttering fevers
Which each new face must give a roving fancy,
When he might rid himself at once of all
By a bare Yes. Who would with patience bear
To fret and linger out a single life,
But that the dread of something untried,
Some hazard in a state from whose strict bond
Death only can release, puzzles the will,
And makes us rather choose those ills we have
Than fly to others which we fancy greater?
This last reflection makes us slow and weary,
Filling the dubious mind with dreadful thoughts
Of curtain-lectures, jealousies, and cares
Extravagantly great, entailed on wedlock
Which to avoid, the lover checks his passion,
And, miserable, dies a bachelor.

The Batchelor's Soliloquy

To wed, or not to wed;-that is the question:
Whether 'tis nobler in a man to suffer
The slings and sorrows of that blind young archer;
Or fly to arms against a host of troubles,
And at the altar end them. To woo-to wed-
No more; and by this step to say we end
The heartache, and the thousand hopes and fears
The single suffer-'tis a consummation
Devoutly to be wished. To woo-to wed;-
To wed--perchance repent!-ay, there's the rub;
For in that wedded state, what woes may come
When we have launched upon that untried sea
Must give us pause. There's the respect
That makes celibacy of so long life;
For who would bear the quips and jeers of friends,
The husband's pity, and the coquette's scorn,
The vacant hearth, the solitary cell,
The unshared sorrow, and the void within,
When he himself might his redemption gain
With a fair damsel. Who would beauty shun
To toil and plod over a barren heath;
But that the dread of something yet beyond-
The undiscovered country, from whose bourne
No bachelor returns-puzzles the will,
And makes us rather bear those ills we have
Than fly to others that we know not of!
Thus forethought does make cowards of us all,
And thus the native hue of resolution
Is sicklied o'er with the pale cast of thought,
And numberless flirtations, long pursued,
With this regard, their currents turn awry
And lose the name of marriage.

Anon

On Your Wedding Day

Today is a day you will always remember
The greatest in anyone's life
You'll start off the day just two people in love
And end it as Husband and Wife

It's a brand new beginning the start of a journey
With moments to cherish and treasure
And although there'll be times when you both disagree
These will surely be outweighed by pleasure

You'll have heard many words of advice in the past
When the secrets of marriage were spoken
But you know that the answers lie hidden inside
Where the bond of true love lies unbroken

So live happy forever as lovers and friends
It's the dawn of a new life for you
As you stand there together with love in your eyes
From the moment you whisper "I do"

And with luck, all your hopes, and your dreams can be real
May success find it's way to your hearts
Tomorrow can bring you the greatest of joys
But today is the day it all starts.

A Bride's Farewell

Goodbye each room, each sunny nook
Where I have lived my days.
Goodbye, before I close the door
Upon my girlhood ways.
With eyes made dim by tender tears
That joy and sorrow tell
I look my last upon the past
My dear old home farewell.

The Dr Prescribes

A lady lately, that was fully sped
Off all the pleasures of the marriage-bed
Ask'd a physician, whether were more fit
For venus' sports, the morning or the night?
The good old man made answer, as 'twas meet,
The morn more wholesome, but the night more sweet.
Nay then, I'faith, quoth she, since we have leisure,
We'll to't each morn for health, each night for pleasure.

The Maid's longing

A maiden of late
Whose name was Sweet Kate,
She dwelt in London near Aldersgate;
Now list to my ditty, declare it I can,
She would have a child without help of a man.

To a doctor she came,
A man of great fame,
Whose deep skill in physick report did proclaim.
Quoth she: "Mr Doctor, shew me if you can
How I may conceive without help of a man."

"Then listen," quoth he,
"Since it must be,
This wonderous strange med'cine I'll shew presently;
Take nine pound of thunder, six legs of a swan,
And you shall conceive without help of a man.

Anon

The love of false harlots,
The faith of false varlets,
With the truth of decoys that walk in their scarlet,
And the feathers of lobster, well fry'd in a pan,
And you shall conceive without help of a man.

Nine drops of rain
Brought hither from Spain,
With the blast of a bellows quite over the main,
With eight quarts of brimstone brew'd in a can,
And you shall conceive without help of a man.

Six pottle of lard,
Squeeze'd from rock hard,
With nine turkey eggs, each as long as a yard,
With pudding of hailstones well bak'd in a pan,
And you shall conceive without help of a man.

These med'cines are good,
And approved have stood,
Well temper'd together with a pottle of blood
Squeez'd fom a grasshopper and the nail of a swan,
To make maids conceive without help of a man."

Solomon Grundy

Solomon Grundy,
Born on a Monday,
Christened on Tuesday,
Married on Wednesday,
Took ill on Thursday,
Grew worse on Friday,
Died on Saturday,
Buried on Sunday.
That was the end of
Solomon Grundy.

On Miss Arabella Young

Here lies, returned to clay
Miss Arabella Young,
Who on the first of May
Began to hold her tongue.

A Wife's Epitaph

To follow you I'm not content.
How do I know which way you went?

Wine & Song

The Drunk

He grabbed me by my slender neck
I couldn't yell or scream.
He took me to his dingy room
Where we could not be seen.
He stripped me of my flimsy wrap,
And gazed upon my form.
I was wet and cold and damp,
And he was nice and warm.
His feverish lips he pressed to mine,
I gave him every drop.
He drained me of my very self,
And I couldn't make him stop.
He made me what I am today,
That's why you find me here...
A broken bottle, tossed away,
That once was full of beer.

The Irish Pig

'Twas an evening in November,
As I very well remember,
I was strolling down the street in drunken pride,
But my knees were all aflutter,
So I landed in the gutter,
And a pig came up and lay down by my side.

Yes, I lay there in the gutter
Thinking thoughts I could not utter,
When a colleen* passing by did softly say,
'Ye can tell a man that boozes
By the company he chooses.' –
At that the pig got up and walked away!

*Generic Irish word for 'girl' also Cailín

Anon

Inscribed On A Pint Pot

There are several reasons for drinking,
And one has just entered my head;
If a man cannot drink when he's living
How the Hell can he drink when he's dead?

Liquor And Longevity

The horse and mule live thirty years
And nothing know of wines and beers.
The goat and sheep at twenty die
And never taste of Scotch or Rye.
The cow drinks water by the ton
And at eighteen is mostly done.
The dog at fifteen cashes in
Without the aid of rum and gin.
The cat in milk and water soaks
And then in twelve short years it croaks.
The modest, sober, bone-dry hen
Lays eggs for nogs, then dies at ten.
All animals are strictly dry:
They sinless live and swiftly die;
But sinful, ginful rum-soaked men
Survive for three score years and ten.
And some of them, a very few,
Stay pickled till they're ninety-two.

In Vino Veritas

In Vino Veritas they say,
Yet lying is so much the custom
Of certain folk, the safest way

The Village Blacksmith

Under the spreading chestnut tree
The village blacksmith stands
The smith an awful cad is he
With very dirty hands
For keepers and the rural police
He doesn't care a hang
He swears and fights, and whops his wife
Gets drunk whene'er he can
In point of fact, our village smith's
A very awful man.

He goes on Sundays to the pub
With other festive boys
When drinking beer and goes of rum
His precious time employs
Till he gets drunk, and going home
He makes no end of noise
Then, with his poor half-starving wife
He in a passion flies
He pulls her by the hair, from off
The bed on which she lies
And kicks her round the room, and says
Bad things about her eyes.

Smoking, soaking, bullying
Onward through life he goes
Each morning sees a blackened eye
Or else a broken nose
I fear that within the County Goal
Calcraft* his life will close
Thanks, thanks to thee, thou black blacksmith
For the lessons thou hast taught
By Calcraft, or his deputy
I never will be caught
And to that end I'll never do
The thing I hadn't ought.

* Calcraft was the official executioner   from 1829 to 1879

Anon

Ballad Of Lydia Pinkham

Let us sing (let us sing) of Lydia Pinkham
The benefactress of the human race.
She invented a vegetable compound,
And now all papers print her face,

O, Mrs. Brown could do no housework,
O, Mrs. Brown could do no housework,
She took three bottles of Lydia's conpound,
And now there's nothing she will shirk,
she will shirk,

Mrs. Jones she had no children,
And she loved them very dear.
So she took three bottles of Pinkham's
Now she has twins every year.

Lottie Smyth ne'er had a lover,
Blotchy pimples caused her plight;
But she took nine bottles of Pinkham's-
Sweethearts swarm about her each night.

Oh Mrs. Murphy (Oh Mrs. Murphy)
Was perturbed because she couldn't seem to pee
Till she took some of Lydia's compound
And now they run a pipeline to the sea!

And Peter Whelan (Peter Whelan)
He was sad because he only had one nut
Till he took some of Lydia's compound
And now they grow in clusters 'round his butt.

Polly Perkins

I am a broken-hearted milkman, in grief I'm arrayed,
Through keeping of the company of a young servant maid,
Who lived on board and wages the house to keep clean
In a gentleman's family near Paddington Green

Chorus:
She was as beautiful as a butterfly
And as proud as a Queen
Was pretty little Polly Perkins of
Paddington Green

She'd an ankle like an antelope and a step like a deer,
A voice like a blackbird, so mellow and clear,
Her hair hung in ringlets so beautiful and long,
I thought that she loved me but I found I was wrong.

When I'd rattle in a morning and cry "milk below",
At the sound of my milk-cans her face she would show
With a smile upon her countenance and a laugh in her eye,
If I thought she'd have loved me, I'd have laid down to die.

When I asked her to marry me she said "Oh! What stuff",
And told me to 'drop it, for she had quite enough
Of my nonsense' – at the same time I'd been very kind,
But to marry a milkman she didn't feel inclined.

"Oh, the man that has me must have silver and gold,
A chariot to ride in and be handsome and bold,
His hair must be curly as any watch spring,
And his whiskers as big as a brush for clothing."

The words that she uttered went straight through my heart,
I sobbed and sighed, and straight did depart;
With a tear on my eyelid as big as bean,
Bidding good-bye to Polly and Paddington Green.

Anon

In six months she married, - this hard-hearted girl, -
But it was not a Wi-count, and it was not a Nearl,
It was not a 'Baronite', but a shade or two wuss,
It was a bow-legged conductor of a twopenny bus.

We Never Mention Aunt Clara

(Parody on The Picture Turned Towards The Wall)

She used to sing hymns in the old village choir
She taught at the Sunday-school class,
At playing the organ she never would tire
Those dear days are over, alas.

In church at the organ she'd practice each day
While the minister pumped up and down.
His wife caught him pumping the organ one day
And that's why aunt Clara left town.

With presents he tempted and lured her to sin
Her innocent virtue to smirch,
But her honour was strong and she never gave in
Till he gave her the deed to the church.

Chorus: We never mention aunt Clara;
Her picture is turned to the wall.
Though she lives on the French Riviera
Mother says she is dead to us all.

They said that she'd toil by night and by day
She'd have to scrub floors for her bread,
But inside of a week she discovered a way
To earn her board lying in bed.

They told her the wages of sinners was death.
To this my aunt Clara just said
That she'd just as soon die with champagne on her breath,
And pink satin sheets on her bed.

Anon

They said no one cared if she'd ever come back
When she left us her fortune to seek
But the boys in the firehouse painted it black
And the ball team wore mourning that week.

They said that no man would make her his bride
They prophesied children of shame
But she's married three earls and a baron besides
And she hasn't a child to her name.

They said that Hellfire would punish her sin
She'd burn for her carryings-on
But just at the moment she's toasting her skin
On the beaches of Deauville and Cannes.

They said that to garments of sackcloth she'd sink
With ashes to cover her head.
But just at the moment it's ermine and mink
And a diamond tiara instead.

They say that she's sunk in the muck and the mud
But the papers last week showed a snap
Of aunt Clara, at Nice, with a prince of the blood
And a bishop asleep on her lap.

The best things in life always go to the pure
The Sunday school lessons all teach
But I wonder when I see the rotogravure
Of her eighty room shack at the beach.

They say that she's sunken, they say that she fell
From the narrow and virtuous path,
But her French formal gardens are sunken as well
And so is her pink marble bath.

Wine & Song

My poor mother's life has been pious and meek
She drives in a second-hand Ford.
Aunt Clara received, for her birthday, last week
A Rolls-Royce, a Stutz and a Cord.

My mother does all of her housework alone
She has to scrub clothes for her board
It strikes me that virtue's not only its own,
But also its only reward.

Chorus: So we never mention aunt Clara,
But I think that when I grow up tall
I shall live on the French Riviera
And let mother turn me to the wall.

Inspiration & Nonsense

A Naughty Poem

She whispered "Will it hurt me?"
"Of course not" answered he
"It's a very simple process,
You can rely on me."
She said "I'm very frightened,
I've not had this before.
My friend has had it five times
And said it can be sore."
It was growing rather painful
Tears formed in her eyes
It was hurting quite a bit now
It must have been a size.
"Calm yourself" he whispered
His face filled with a grin
"Try and open wider
So I can get it in."
"It's coming now" he whispered
"I know" she cried in bliss
Feeling it deep within her now
She said "I am glad I'm having this."
And with a final effort
She gave a frightened shout
He gripped it in anguish
And quickly pulled it out.
She lay back quite contended
Sighed and gave a smile
She said "I'm glad I came now
You made it worth my while."
Now if you read this carefully
The dentist you will find
Is not what you imagined
It's just your dirty mind!

Anon

Well, hardly Ever

Never throw a brick at a drownin' man
Outside a grocery store –
Always throw him a bar of soap –
And he'll wash himself ashore.

Faults

We men have many faults
Poor women have but two:-
There's nothing good they say;
There's nothing good they do.

Careless Willie

Willie with a thirst for gore
Nailed his sister to the door
Mother said with humor quaint
"Careful, Willie, don't scratch the paint!"

Predestination

We are the precious chosen few:
Let all the rest be damned.
There's only room for one or two:
We can't have Heaven crammed.

My Bishop's Eyes

My Bishop's eyes I've never seen
Though the light in them may shine;
For when he prays he closes his,
And when he preaches, mine.

Tibetan Lament

The loveliest of our lamas
Is gone beyond the door.
He'll never wear pajamas
Any more, any more.

Above the yawning chasm
He tried to pass a yak;
It took a sneezing spasm
And blew him off his track.
Now the silent valley has him,
And he can't come back.

The loveliest of our lamas
Is gone beyond the door.
He'll never wear pajamas
Any more.

Queen Caroline

Most Gracious Queen, we thee implore
To go away and sin no more,
But if that effort be too great,
To go away at any rate.

Cosmic Egg

The Cosmic Egg
Upon a rock yet un-create,
Amid a chaos inchoate,
An uncreated being sate;
Beneath him, rock,
Above him, cloud.
And the cloud was rock,
And the rock was cloud.
The rock then growing soft and warm,
The cloud began to take a form,
A form chaotic, vast and vague,
Which issued in the cosmic egg.
Then the being un-create
On the egg did incubate,
And thus became the incubator;
And of the egg did allegate,
And thus became the alligator;
And the incubator was potentate,
But the alligator was potentator.

God And The Soldier

God and the soldier
All men adore
In time of trouble,
And no more;
For when war is over
And all things righted,
God is neglected -
The old soldier slighted.

Psychiatrist?

So you'll to the Psychiatrist,
Your little psyche's queer?
You need, I think to see a good
Psmackbottomist, my dear!

Susan Simpson

Suddenly swallows swiftly skimming
Sunset's slowly spreading shade,
Silvery songsters sweetly singing
Summer's soothing serenade.

Susan Simpson strolled sedately,
Stifling sobs, suppressing sighs.
Seeing Stephen Slocum, stately
She stopped, showing some surprise.

"Say", said Stephen, "sweetest sigher;
Say, shall Stephen spouseless stay?"
Susan, seeming somewhat shyer,
Showed submissiveness straightaway.

Summer's season slowly stretches,
Susan Simpson Slocum she –
So she signed some simple sketches –
Soul sought soul successfully.

Six Septembers Susan swelters;
Six sharp seasons snow supplies;
Susan's satin sofa shelters
Six small Slocums side by side.

Anon

We're In The Dumps

We're all in the dumps,
For diamonds are trumps;
The kittens are gone to St Paul's!
The babies are bit,
The moon's in a fit,
And the houses are built without walls.

Diodorus Siculus

Diodorus Siculus
Made himself ridiculous
He thought a thimble
Was a phallic symbol.

Jonathan Swift

Jonathan Swift
Never went up in a lift;
Nor did the author of 'Robinson Crusoe'
Do so.

Godfrey Gore

Godfrey Gordon Gustuvus Gore
The boy who'd never shut the door
His Father would Plead and mother implore
Godfrey Gordon Please Shut the door.

The Empress Of Poppea

The Empress of Poppea
Was really rather a dear,
Only no one could stop her
From being improper.

Mrs. Harding

"Parding, Mrs Harding,
Is my kitting in your kitching garding,
Gnawing of a mutting-bone?"
"No, he's gone to Londing."
"Eleving? I thought it was only seving.
Heavings! What a long way from home!"

The Modern Hiawatha

When he killed the Mudjokivis,
Of the skin he made him mittens,
Made them with the fur side inside,
Made them with the skin side outside,
He, to get the warm side inside,
Put the inside skins side outside;
He, to get the cold side outside,
Put the warm side fur side inside.
That is why he put the fur side inside,
Why he put the skin side outside,
Why he turned them inside outside.

Anon

Weather Forecast

The rain it raineth every day,
Upon the just and unjust fella,
But more upon the just, because
The unjust has the just's umbrella.

If All The World Were Paper

If all the world were paper,
And all the sea were inke;
And all the trees were bread and cheese,
What should we do for drinke?

If all the world were sand 'o,
Oh, then what should we lack 'o;
If as they say there were no clay,
How should we make tobacco?

If all our vessels ran 'a,
If none but had a crack 'a;
If Spanish apes eat all the grapes,
What should we do for sack 'a?

If fryers had no bald pates,
Nor nuns had no dark cloysters,
If all the seas were beans and peas,
What should we do for oysters?

If there had been no projects,
Nor none that did great wrongs;
If fiddlers shall turn players all,
What should we do for songs?

If all things were eternal,
And nothing their end bringing;
If this should be, then how should we
Here make an end of singing?

Mr. Nobody

I know a funny little man,
    As quiet as a mouse,
Who does the mischief that is done
    In everybody's house!
There's no one ever sees his face,
    And yet we all agree
That every plate we break was cracked
    By Mr. Nobody.

'Tis he who always tears out books,
    Who leaves the door ajar,
He pulls the buttons from our shirts,
    And scatters pins afar;
That squeaking door will always squeak,
    For prithee, don't you see,
We leave the oiling to be done
    By Mr. Nobody.

The finger marks upon the door
    By none of us are made;
We never leave the blinds unclosed,
    To let the curtains fade.
The ink we never spill; the boots
    That lying round you see
Are not our boots,—they all belong
    To Mr. Nobody.

Festivities

The Reckoning

Now the festive season's ended
Comes the sequel parents dread;
Pale and visibly distended
Bilious Tommy lies in bed,
Face to face with retribution
And an outraged constitution.

What a change since, pink and perky
Tommy swiftly put away
Three enormous goes of turkey
At the feast on Christmas Day,
Getting by judicious bluffing
Double quantities of stuffing.

As to pudding, who could reckon
Tommy's load in terms of size?
Who attempt to keep a check on
Tommy's numberless mince pies?
Hopeless task! His present pallor
Proves his prodigies of valour.

Then I found him, notwithstanding
Such colossal feats as these,
After dinner on the landing
Secretly devouring cheese,
Flanked by ginger-beer-and-coffee,
Sweetened with a slab of toffee.

I, his uncle, gave him warning,
Showed him the error of his ways,
Hinted at tomorrow morning,
Talked about my boyhood days;
All in vain I waved the bogey
He despised me as a fogey.

Well, perhaps the pains he suffers
May be gifts of fairy gold,
Since he now says, 'Only duffers
Eat as much as they can hold.'
Thus, through physic and privations,
Tommy learns his limitations.

For Children Or For Grown-Ups

Tis the week before Christmas and every night
As soon as the children are snuggled up tight
And have sleepily murmured their wishes and prayers,
Such fun as goes on in the parlour downstairs!
For Father, Big Brother, and Grandfather too,
Start in with great vigour their youth to renew.
The Grown-ups are having great fun - all is well;
And they play till it's long past their hour for bed.

They try to solve puzzles and each one enjoys
The magical thrill of mechanical toys,
Even Mother must play with a doll that can talk,
And if you assist it, it's able to walk.
It's really no matter if paint may be scratched,
Or a cogwheel, a nut, or a bolt gets detached;
The grown-ups are having great fun - all is well;
The children don't know it, and Santa won't tell.

I'm A Little Snowman

I'm a little snowman round and fat,
Here are my mittens,
Here is my hat.
Add a little scarf and a carrot nose,
I stand so tall when the cold wind blows

Once There Was A Snowman

Once there was a snowman,
Who stood outside the door,
He wished that he could come inside,
And run about the floor.
He wished that he could warm himself,
Beside the fire, so red,
He wished that he could climb
Upon the big white bed.
So he called to the North Wind,
"Come and help me, pray,
For I'm completely frozen,
Standing here all day."
So the North Wind came along,
And blew him in the door,
And now there nothing left,
But a puddle on the floor!

Anon

Funny Face

The funniest face
Looked out at me
From a silver ball
On the Christmas Tree!
At first I thought
It was Santa's elf,
But I looked again and
It was just myself!

Christmas Eve

We have been helping with the cake,
And licking out the pan,
And wrapping up our packages,
As neatly as we can.
We have hung our stockings up,
Beside the open grate.
And now there's nothing more to do,
Except
To
Wait.

Santa's New Idea

Said Santa Claus
One winter's night,
"I really think it's only right
That gifts should have a little say
'Bout where they'll be on Christmas Day."
So then and there
He called the toys
Intended for good girls and boys,
And when they'd settled down to hear,
He made his plan for them quite clear.
These were his words:
"Soon now," he said,
"You'll all be speeding off with me
To being the Christmas joy and cheer
To little ones both far and near.
Here's my idea,
It seems but fair
That you should each one have a share
In choosing homes where you will stay
On and after Christmas Day.
Now the next weeks
Before we go
Over the miles of glistening snow
Find out the tots that you like best
And think much nicer than the rest."
The toys called out
"Hurrah! Hurrah!
What fun to live always and play
With folks we choose – they'll surely be
Selected very carefully."
So, children dear,
When you do see
Your toys in socks or on a tree,
You'll know in all the world 'twas you
They wanted to be given to.

Christmas Presents

Every year Grandma gets a tin of talcum powder.
She always says, "Ah my favourite!"
Even before she opens the wrapping
Grandpa always says, "Well, I know what's in here.
Its two pairs of socks. Just what I wanted!"
This year, Auntie Vi had an umbrella in an umbrella-shaped parcel,
I mean, it looked just like an umbrella.
And, before Auntie Vi pulled the paper off,
She said to Mum, "It will match that new coat of mine."
As for Mum and Dad, they just sat there and said,
"We've given each other a joint present this year
It's a digital clock radio for our bedroom."
Do you know, they didn't even bother to wrap it up and put it under the
tree!
At the end, when everything had been given out,
Mum said, "We mustn't forget the gift-vouchers from Debbie and Jim.
We sent them a cheque for the same amount.
We always do."
I call that a bit unimaginative, don't you?
Maybe, when you come to think about it,
Grown-ups need Father Christmas far more than children do.

Food

New Sights

I like to see a thing I know
Has not been seen before;
That's why I cut my apple through
To look into the core.

It's nice to think, though many an eye
Has seen the ruddy skin,
Mine is the very first to spy
The five brown pips within.

I Asked The Maid

I asked the maid in dulcet tone
To order me a buttered scone.
The silly girl has been and gone
And ordered me a buttered scone.

Peas

I always eat peas with honey
I've done it all my life
It makes the peas taste funny
But it keeps them on the knife

Anon

Don't Ask For Bread

A wretched man walked up and down
To buy his dinner in the town.
At last he found a wretched place
And entered in with modest grace,

Took off his coat, took off his hat,
And wiped his feet upon the mat,
Took out his purse to count his pence
And found he had but two half-cents.

The bill of fare, he scanned it through
To see what two half-cents would do.
The only item of them all
For two half-cents was one fishball.

So to the waiter he did call
And gently whispered: One fishball
The waiter bellowed down the hall;
"This gentleman here wants one fishball."

The diners looked both one and all
To see who wanted one fishball.
The wretched man, all ill at ease
Said: "A little bread, sir, if you please."

The waiter bellowed down the hall:
"We don't serve bread with one fishball."
The wretched man, he felt so small,
He quickly left the dining hall.

The wretched man he went outside
And shot himself until he died.
This is the moral of it all,
Don't ask for bread with one fishball.

Do You Carrot All For Me?

Do you carrot all for me?
My heart beets for you,
With your turnip nose
And your radish face.
You are a peach.
If we cantaloupe,
Lettuce marry;
Weed make a swell pear.

Cheese Mites

The cheese-mites asked how the cheese got there,
And warmly debated the matter;
The orthodox said it came from the air,
And the heretics said from the platter.

King Arthur

When good King Arthur ruled the land,
He was a goodly king:
He stole three pecks of barley meal,
To make a bag-pudding.

A bag-pudding the king did make,
And stuffed it well with plums;
And in it put great lumps of fat,
As big as my two thumbs.

The king and queen did eat thereof,
And noblemen beside;
And what they could not eat that night,
The queen next morning fried.

Anon

The Virtues Of Carnation Milk

Carnation milk is the best in the land:
Here I sit with a can in my hand –
No tits to pull, no hay to pitch,
You just punch a hole in the son of a bitch.

Look Out Tummy

Through the teeth
And past the gums
Look out tummy
Here it comes

Mushrooms

The mushroom is a vegetable
To select it few are able
You won't know them when you meet them
You won't know them 'til you eat them
If in heaven you awaken
You will know you were mistaken
And the ones that you have eaten
Weren't the ones you should have et.

Grub Up

I wish I was a little grub
With whiskers round my tummy.
I'd climb into a honey pot
And make my tummy gummy.

On Nevski Bridge

On Nevski Bridge a Russian stood
Chewing his beard for lack of food
Said he, 'It's tough this stuff to eat
But a darn sight better than shredded wheat!'

Mother Nature

The Doggies Meeting

The doggies held a meeting,
They came from near and far,
Some came by motor cycle,
And some by motor car
Each doggie passed the doorway,
Each doggie signed the book
Each one unshipped his asshole
And hung it on a hook.

One dog was not invited
It sorely raised his ire
He ran into the meeting hall
And loudly shouted "Fire!"
It threw them in confusion
And without a second look
Each grabbed another's asshole
From off another hook

And that's the reason why sir,
When walking down the street
And that's the reason why sir,
When doggies chance to meet
And that's the reason why sir,
On land, abroad or home
They'll sniff each other's backside...
To see if it's their own.

Anon

The Mighty Oak

Don't worry if your job is small,
And your rewards are few.
Remember that the mighty oak,
Was once a nut like you.

The Frog

What a wonderful bird the frog are!
When he stand he sit almost;
When he hop he fly almost.
He ain't got no sense hardly;
He ain't got no tail hardly either.
When he sit, he sit on what he ain't got almost.

The Pin

As Nature H – y's Clay was blending,
Uncertain what her work should end in,
Whether in female or in male,
A Pin dropped in, and turned the scale.

The Secret

We have a secret, just we three,
The robin, and I, and the sweet cherry-tree;
The bird told the tree, and the tree told me,
And nobody knows it but just us three.

But of course the robin knows it best,
Because she built the - I shan't tell the rest;
And laid the four little - something in it -
I'm afraid I shall tell it every minute.

But if the tree and the robin don't peep,
I'll try my best the secret to keep;
Though I know when the little birds fly about
Then the whole secret will be out.

Quick Quick

Quick!   quick!
  The cat's been sick.

Where?   where?
  Under the chair.

Hasten!   hasten!
  Fetch the basin.

Alack!   alack!
  It is too late,
The carpet's in
  An awful state.

No!   no!
  It's all in vain,
For she has licked it
  Up again.

Anon

Gay Birds

Cuckoos lead Bohemian lives,
They fail as husbands and as wives,
And so they cynically disparage
Everybody else's marriage.

To The Moon

Oh Moon, when I look on thy beautiful face,
Careering along through the boundaries of space,
The thought has quite frequently come to my mind,
If ever I'll gaze on thy glorious behind.

Cormorant

The common cormorant or shag
Lays eggs inside a paper bag.
The reason you will see no doubt
It is to keep the lightning out.
But what these unobservant birds
Have never noticed is that herds
Of wandering bears may come with buns
And steal the bags to hold the crumbs

Mary Had A Little Lamb

Mary had a little lamb,
She ate it with mint sauce,
And everywhere that Mary went
The lamb went too, of course.

Mary Had A Little Crocodile

Mary had a little crocodile
That ate a child each day
But interfering people came
And took her pet away.

Mary Had A Little Lamb (Again)

Mary had a little lamb,
She thought it was quite silly.
She threw it up into the air,
And caught it by its ...
Willy was a watch dog,
Lying on the grass.
Down came a bumble bee,
And bit him on the ...
Asssssk no questions,
Tell no lies,
I saw a policeman,
Doing up his ...
Flies are bad,
Mosquitos are worse,
And this is the end of my silly little verse.

Way Down South

Way down South where bananas grow,
A grasshopper stepped on an elephant's toe.
The elephant said, with tears in his eyes,
"Pick on somebody your own size."

Anon

Sex Life Of A Camel

Oh, the sexual life of the camel
Is stranger than anyone thinks.
In moments of amorous passion,
He frequently buggers the Sphinx.

But the Sphinx's posterior passage
Is clogged with the sands of the Nile,
Which accounts for the hump on the camel,
And the Sphinx's inscrutable smile.

A Flea And A Fly

A flea and a fly in a flue
Were imprisoned, so what could they do?
Said the fly: "Let us flee"
Said the flea: "Let us fly!"
So they flew through a flaw in the flue.

The Rabbit

The rabbit has a charming face:
Its private life is a disgrace.
I really dare not name to you
The awful things that rabbits do;
Things that your paper never prints –
You only mention them in hints.
They have such lost, degraded souls
No wonder they inhabit holes;
When such depravity is found
It only can live underground.

Algy Met A Bear

Algy met a bear.
The bear met Algy
The bear was bulgy
The bulge was Algy

If You Should Meet A Crocodile

If you should meet a crocodile,
Don't take a stick and poke him;
Ignore the welcome in his smile,
Be careful not to stroke him.
For as he sleeps upon the Nile,
He thinner gets and thinner;
But whene'er you meet a crocodile
He's ready for his dinner.

Wise Old Owl

A wise old owl sat in an oak,
The more he heard the less he spoke;
The less he spoke the more he heard.
Why aren't we all like that wise old bird?

Anon

Lines By A Humanitarian

Be lenient with lobsters, and ever kind to crabs,
And be not disrespectful to cuttle-fish or dabs;
Chase not the Cochin-China, chaff not the ox obese,
And babble not of feather-beds in company with geese.
Be tender with the tadpole, and let the limpet thrive,
Be merciful to mussels, don't skin your eels alive;
When talking to a turtle don't mention calipee —
Be always kind to animals wherever you may be.

The Hunter

I have fought against the poodle with his gory, deadly paws;
I have faced the fearsome kitten, wild and bony,
And somehow I've evaded the enormous chomping jaws
Of the frighteningly ferocious Shetland pony.

My triumph o'er the rabbit is now sung throughout the land,
And men still speak in whispers of the day
When, attacked by twelve mosquitoes, with my one unwounded hand,
I killed nine of them and dove the rest away.

I have faced the housefly in his lair, I have stalked the ladybug
And the caterpillar, grim and fierce and hairy;
That trophy there is bumblebee, and this, my favourite rug,
Has been fashioned from the hide of a canary.

I have dove into the ocean to do combat with a shrimp,
I have dared the hen to come on out and fight;
I have battled with the butterfly (that's why I have this limp),
And I slew a monstrous grubworm just last night.

But this evening I must sally forth to meet the savage moth,
And if I don't come back in time for tea,
You shall know that I fell gallantly, as gallantly I fought
So please be gentle when you speak of me.

If you've enjoyed reading **Anon** - don't keep it to yourself, please consider leaving an honest review on *Amazon, Goodreads* or any other literary outlet you frequent. It's good karma to share and it helps to make the world a better place for all.

Also if you have any comments about how this book could be improved, or if you have any suggestions for a potential future poetry book project for *TAP Publishing UK*, please get in touch via the website contact page www.tappublishing.uk/contact-tapp/ or alternatively by sending an e-mail to information@tappublishing.com. Your feedback is important and most welcome.

About

The Editor

David Sollis was born and raised in South Wales, but moved to England in 1991, where he now lives with his wife, two children, two goldfish and a rabbit. He has been reading and writing poetry since childhood and has a particular penchant for rhyming forms - especially light-verse, limericks and parody. He publishes some of his own writings and illustrations on his blog www.tappublishing.uk/blog. But, perhaps due to a lack of confidence or a generous portion of false modesty, he has no ambitions to publish a book of his own poems. Instead he chooses to concentrate his efforts on compiling and publishing anthologies of other poet's works.

All Said & Done [ISBN 978-0-9573175-0-5] was David's first poetry anthology, published in 2012 to raise funds for the *National Autistic Society* (the UK's leading autism charity). This unique anthology contains a veritable smörgåsbord of the best in light verse that will have you laughing out loud, or at the very least, raise a wry smile. Throughout the book there are also some more poignant and thought provoking pieces. The poems have been chosen to provide a snapshot of modern life and cover topics we're all familiar with (e.g. Relationships, Communication and Empathy). It is no coincidence that these themes encompass some of the main areas of difficulty for autistic individuals. The collection contains poems written by the famous and not so famous, both autistic and non-autistic poets from all over the English speaking world.

David is also founder of *The Amorphous Poetry Project* (TAPP) and its publishing outlet *TAP Publishing UK*. Started with a vision of helping people connect with their frustrated poets within, be creative, have fun and raise money for charity.

You can find out more about TAPP by visiting: www.tappublishing.uk.

It is highly recommended when you visit the website that you sign-up to the e-mail newsletter so that you can keep up-to-date with:

- Giveaways
- Time limited special offers and discounts
- Competitions
- Forthcoming publications and works in progress

Don't worry, your details will not be shared with any third parties. Nor will we inundate your inbox every other day. We will only issue a newsletter when we have something worthwhile to share.

You can also submit your poems for possible inclusion in future published anthologies. By e-mailing them to submissions@tappublishing.uk Please ensure that you first familiarize yourself with TAPP's submission guidelines available on the website www.tappublishing.uk/submission/.

Don't be a stranger – your all welcome – the more the merrier.

Long live The Amorphous Poetry Project and god bless all who wail with her…

21st Century Verse
COMING SOON!